CW00401114

Teacher's Notes
Roman Britain

Isabel Macdonald

Series editor | Sue Palmer

Contents

OXFORD
UNIVERSITY PRESS

Great Clarendon Street, Oxford OX2 6DP

Oxford University Press is a department of the University of Oxford.
It furthers the University's objective of excellence in research, scholarship,
and education by publishing worldwide in

Oxford New York

Auckland Bangkok Buenos Aires Cape Town Chennai
Dar es Salaam Delhi Hong Kong Istanbul Karachi Kolkata
Kuala Lumpur Madrid Melbourne Mexico City Mumbai Nairobi
São Paulo Shanghai Taipei Tokyo Toronto

Oxford is a registered trade mark of Oxford University Press
in the UK and in certain other countries

British Library Cataloguing in Publication Data

Data available

ISBN 019 834867 3

3 5 7 9 10 8 6 4 2

Typeset by Fakenham Photosetting, Fakenham, Norfolk

Printed in the UK

What is Oxford Connections?

Oxford Connections is a set of 12 cross-curricular books and related teaching materials for 7 to 11 year olds. The books will help you teach literacy through a science, geography or history-based topic. Each book provides the material to cover one unit from the QCA Schemes of Work for the National Curriculum in England and Wales, and the non-fiction literacy objectives for one whole year of the National Literacy Strategy. (You can find a grid of where the QCA and NLS objectives are covered on p 48 of these notes and on the inside back cover of the pupils' books.) The books can be used to focus primarily on literacy or on science/geography/history.

Literacy

Pupils need different literacies. As well as traditional texts with different purposes and audiences, they also need to be able to understand and write material presented in different forms such as diagrams, bullet points, notes and Internet displays, particularly when working with non-fiction.

Oxford Connections supports the development of these different literacies. It focuses particularly on reading and writing non-fiction, and will help pupils use effectively the different non-fiction text types (report, explanation, instructions, recount, discussion, persuasion).

Using these books will help pupils to focus on the two main elements which make a text type what it is:

◆ The language features used (for example, present tense for instructions, and past tense for recounts, use of commands in instructions etc.).
◆ The structure of the text (for example, chronological order, in the case of instructions or recounts).

The structure of a text can be represented as a diagram or framework, showing visually how the parts of the text fit together, which are the main points and how they are developed. (A very common example of this type of presentation is a timeline, which shows events that have happened in the past, as a continuum, the order of which cannot change.) In this book, we refer to material presented in this diagrammatic way as *visual* (*visual reports, visual explanations*, etc.).

Pupils will learn to read and to present information visually (by using frameworks), thus developing good note-taking skills, and consolidating their understanding of how texts are structured. The visual texts in particular are accessible to those pupils who need more support. Using frameworks to plan their own writing will also help improve all pupils' planning and drafting/editing skills.

In this book, we have used icons to represent the different sorts of frameworks you can use, called *skeletons*. These are referred to in the *National Literacy Strategy Support Materials for Text Level Objectives* (DfES 0532/2001). They can be used as an aide-memoir to help pupils remember the structure of each text type. They appear on pp 6–47 to show you what text types are on the pupils' book pages.

Recount		Explanation	
Instructions		Persuasion	
Non-chronological report		Discussion	

Using *Roman Britain* to teach literacy

There are step-by-step instructions to teach pupils how to read and write the different text types on pp 18–47 (a six-page section for each text type). They follow this model:

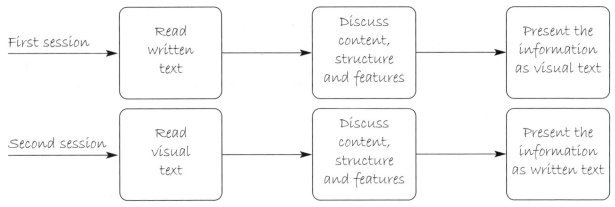

Each six-page section contains:

Two pages of step-by-step instructions taking you through the process described in the diagram above. They will help you analyse a written text, and then produce a visual version of that text with a group of pupils. You will then analyse a visual text, producing a written version.

A page describing the relevant text type.*

An example of the text type (an excerpt from *Roman Britain* pupils' book) for you to read and analyse with pupils.*

The same example with language features highlighted for your reference.*

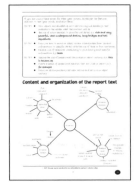

A visual version of the written text for your reference.*

These can be photocopied as handouts, a poster or an OHT.

There are page-by-page notes on how to use the material to cover other aspects of literacy on pp 6–17. These page-by-page notes also show how to use the material in the pupils' book for the particular subject, e.g. history. You can also find a grid showing where the literacy objectives are covered on p 48 of these notes, and on the inside back cover of the *Roman Britain* pupils' book.

Speaking and listening, and drama

The discussion which is inherent in this method of learning should improve pupils' speaking and listening skills. As well as helping pupils to organize and structure their ideas before writing, visual texts should prompt pupils to use the relevant language features orally. Additional speaking and listening, and drama activities such as those below, can be used to further reinforce the pupils' learning.

Retelling – taking a section from a visual recount and retelling the events either individually or in groups.

Role play – using the visuals created by the whole class to ask/answer questions in role as the person in the recount or by taking one side of the argument.

Mini plays – retelling an event or following an explanation visual to show how something works. Pupils could be the different parts of whatever is being explained.

Puppet plays – retelling an event or following an explanation visual.

Freeze-frame – showing sections from a recount visual or report visual. Pupils could work in groups to show different aspects of a discussion.

TV/radio reports – demonstrating knowledge using a visual report as a TV/radio report. In a TV report images could be used either pictorially or by the use of freeze-framing.

TV demonstrations – following an instruction visual or explanation visual to demonstrate how to make something or explain how something works.

TV/radio interviews – retelling events in recounts or using report visuals while interviewing another pupil/pupils in role.

TV/radio adverts – using a persuasive visual to make adverts.

Illustrated talks – using the visual as a prompt.

Hot seat – answering questions in role – either as a persuasion, report or recount.

Debates – using discussion visuals to have debates between individuals or groups.

Using *Roman Britain* to teach History

Roman Britain contains all the material you need to cover this topic, and to achieve the objectives of the *QCA Scheme of Work for the National Curriculum History Unit 6a* (recommended for Year 3 pupils). There are page-by-page notes on how to use the material for history on pp 6–17. You can find a grid showing how the QCA objectives are covered on p 48 of these notes, and on the inside back cover of *Roman Britain* pupils' book.

Which year group should I use *Roman Britain* with?

Roman Britain has been written for Year 3 pupils (7–8 year olds). However, if your school places the topic in another year group, the history material contained in *Roman Britain* will still be suitable for use with other age groups. Although all of the non-fiction literacy objectives for Year 3 are covered, many of the objectives for other year groups are also supported. Most of the six non-fiction text types are covered in it, and language features for Years 4, 5 and 6 are highlighted in the relevant sections.

NB throughout this introduction the term *Year 3* has been used to mean 7–8 year olds. The references in the grid on p 48 are to the *National Literacy Strategy* and to the *QCA Scheme of Work for the National Curriculum*. However, *Roman Britain* is suitable for use with P4 in Scotland and in Northern Ireland, since it supports many elements of the *National Guidelines, 5–14* and *The Northern Ireland Curriculum*. The history content of *Roman Britain* does not conflict in any way with either *National Guidelines, 5–14* or *The Northern Ireland Curriculum*.

SCOTLAND
AND NORTHERN
IRELAND

Pages 2–3

History

Use these pages as advance organizers to provide pupils with an overview of the work to be conducted:

Concept map shows the main areas to be covered and the links between them.

Contents page shows how this information has been organized in the book.

- ◆ Use the quotation as an aid for using the Contents page – ask the pupils to find the topic mentioned.
- ◆ Return to the pages occasionally during teaching to help the pupils see how their learning and understanding is building up.
- ◆ Use as a revision aid, asking pupils to summarize what they know about each aspect.
- ◆ Use the Concept map at the end of the topic to review all areas of the topic covered.

Literacy

Help pupils to recognize the similarities and differences between the concept map and contents page:

- ◆ they contain the same information, but are organized differently
- ◆ Concept map provides an overview of the ideas contained in the book and how they are interlinked; the Contents page provides a linear guide to the way these ideas are organized
- ◆ *Contents page* gives page numbers for ease of reference.

Throughout your use of the book, demonstrate how to use the contents page – along with the index (see p 17 of these notes) – to access information when required.

Pages 4–5

History

Key concept
- ◆ Understand that the Romans and Celts lived a long time ago.

Key vocabulary
- ◆ *ancient, ruins, excavation, artefact, before Christ (BC), after Christ (AD) – anno domini = the year of our Lord*

Suggested activities
- ◆ Pupils, in pairs, discuss pictures of Roman buildings and identify features and evidence that suggest the buildings are from an ancient culture.
- ◆ Groups of pupils discuss pictures of buildings across the ages, including Roman and Celtic, and place them on a line of chronology from oldest to most recent. Discuss the reasons for the ordering.

Literacy

page 4	page 5
written report	written report

These pages are used a featured example to teach pupils how to read and write **report** texts. See pp 18–23 of these teacher's notes.

- ◆ Use also to encourage pupils to structure their research using the questions e.g. *What do we know about the Romans? What else would we like to know? Where will we find this out?*
- ◆ Make an OHT of p 4 and demonstrate to pupils how to summarize their understanding by text marking to identify key words and phrases then writing short notes based on them, recording on whiteboards.
- ◆ Identify further sources e.g. *library, web pages, museums,* to find evidence about the Romans.

History

Key concept

◆ Understand the terms 'invade' and 'settle'.

Key vocabulary

◆ *invader, settler, invasion, empire, conquer, emperor*

Suggested activities

◆ Stage a mock invasion – one class or group to another. With invading class, discuss the rules they will impose upon the other class etc. After invasion, discuss how the other class felt when they were invaded.

◆ Pupils record their thoughts and refer these back to the countries that were invaded by the Romans.

Literacy

page 6	page 7
visual report	visual report

Use these pages to show pupils how to organize information found on maps (Link to Geography), making skeleton notes to use to produce a non-chronological report about the subject.

◆ On a whiteboard, create a table or information chart about the Romans using categories such as: *Countries ruled by Rome; crops grown; goods traded.*

◆ Use map to demonstrate to pupils how to skim and scan for information such as *Which countries were in the Empire?*

◆ Pupils use information on chart to create skeleton for report text. Then, using the chart headings as their paragraph headings, write their own report about the Roman Empire.

History

Key concept

◆ To place the main events of the Roman and Celtic periods in chronological framework.

Key vocabulary

◆ *ancient, modern,* AD, BC, *year, century*

Suggested activities

◆ Create a large timeline in the classroom that includes recent history relevant to pupils e.g. births, school opening, parent, grandparents, birth, known periods in History already covered e.g. Fire of London etc. Include BC /AD.

◆ Explain terms BC and AD. Link to the birth of Christ. (Link to RE) Include other persons known to pupils e.g. 1952 reign of our Queen begins.

◆ Make cards with the main dates and events of Roman Empire timeline (pp 8–9). In pairs, pupils place these in the correct chronological order. Add key dates to main class timeline. Highlight the distance between Roman times and the present.

Literacy

page 8	page 9
visual recount	visual recount

Use these pages to help pupils use this visual recount to find the key information about the Roman Empire.

◆ Discuss the key points in the Roman timeline and encourage pupils to group events into sections.

◆ In pairs, pupils discuss the visual recount of the Roman Empire and identify key points in its history, writing notes to create their own recount skeletons.

◆ To practise speaking and listening skills, combine the oral news reports with still pictures or freeze frames to create a dramatic recount of events. (Link to Drama)

◆ Pupils write own recount of the Rise and Fall of the Roman Empire using their skeleton notes.

History

Key concepts

◆ Use the terms 'invade' and 'settle'.
◆ To know that the Romans invaded and a period of conquest was followed by a period of settlement.

Key vocabulary

◆ *soldier, efficient, organized, comrades, profession, trained, invade, conquest, rule, conquer*

Suggested activities

◆ Stage a recruiting day where each pupil has to persuade a commanding officer (teacher) to let him join the army. Pupils prepare reasons using information in these pages. Focus on pupils giving reasons using extended sentences e.g. I should join the Roman army *because* . . .
◆ Give pupils cards showing a series of statements containing both true and false facts about the army. Ask pupils to sort them into 'true' and 'false' and cite different sources as evidence for their decision.
◆ Create an annotated diagram giving information about the Roman soldiers.
◆ Pupils create posters advertising the greatness of the Roman armies as successful invaders.

Literacy

page 10	page 11
visual report	visual report

These pages are used as a featured example to teach pupils how to read and write **report** texts. See pp 18–23 of these teacher's notes.

History

Key concepts

◆ To make comparisons between Roman and Celtic lifestyles.
◆ To learn about aspects of Roman and Celtic life using a variety of resources.

Key vocabulary

◆ *tunic, armour, helmet, breast plate, shield, cloak, tunic, torc, woad, similarity, difference*

Suggested activities

◆ Compare and contrast the costume of a Roman soldier and a Celtic warrior by dressing two pupils up, one as a Roman and one as a Celt.
◆ Make Roman and Celtic shields that serve the same purpose but remain true to the two cultures (Link to DT/Maths/Art)
◆ Pupils use the descriptions on the pages to make a collages/paintings of a Celtic warrior.
◆ Use plants to create dye and explore dying small pieces of material (Link to DT).

Literacy

Page 12	Page 13
visual comparative report	visual comparative report

These pages are used as a featured example to teach pupils how to read and write **comparative report** texts. See pp 24–29 of these teacher's notes

◆ Use also to create a glossary of words identified in the text and organize alphabetically.

History

Key concept

◆ To learn about aspects of Celtic and Roman life in Britain.

Key vocabulary

◆ *druids, clan chiefs, bards, slaves, craft workers*

Suggested activities

◆ Through role play, pupils create freeze frames of the different roles of the Celtic community. Pupils in role explain their role in the community. (Link to Drama) On cards, write name and descriptions of the jobs of different people in the Celtic community. In pairs, pupils sort the statements to match the correct person.

◆ Use clay to make simple pots with a Celtic design. (Link to Art/sculpture)

Literacy

page 14	page 15
written report	visual report

Use p 14 to teach pupils to identify the main points of the text or paragraph.

◆ Using OHP, demonstrate to pupils how to text mark to find three key facts about the Celts from first section e.g. how to convert facts into these notes: *Settled in Britain 1000 BC and 100 BC; lived in tribes; overpowered people already living here.*

◆ In pairs, pupils then read the second section and identify key words/ facts by text marking then make notes.

◆ Discuss how their skeleton notes should be written: i.e. not complete sentences; key words that may be organized into phrases for sense.

◆ In pairs, pupils orally summarize the key facts they now know about the Celts using their notes as a prompt.

◆ Use pictures on p 15 as basis for visual report skeleton. Point out that the organization of the pictures show the structure of Celtic communities i.e. Kings on top.

History

Key concept

◆ To learn about aspects of life in Roman and Celtic Britain.

Key vocabulary

◆ *torc, woad, pattern, belief*

Suggested activities

◆ Follow the instructions on p 16 to make a Celtic torc. (Link to DT)

◆ Pupils using compasses, make their own Celtic designs for shields. (Link to Art QCA Unit 3b.)

◆ Discuss the Celtic belief that painted patterns and woad would protect them from harm – link to other religions and their beliefs and customs. e.g. Muslims – always take shoes off in mosque, don't eat bacon; for Hindus the cow is sacred etc. (Link to RE QCA Unit 3a.)

Literacy

Page 16	Page 17
written instructions	written report

These pages are a used as a featured example to teach pupils how to read and write **instruction** texts. See pp 36–41 of these teacher's notes.

History

Key concept
◆ Learn about aspects of life in Celtic and Roman Britain, using a variety of resources.

Key vocabulary
◆ *wattle, daub, quern, loom, sickle*

Suggested activities
◆ Experiment with grinding wheat grains into flour using two stones acting like a quern.
◆ Pupils create similar structures to Celtic farms on a miniature scale using sticks and clay etc to act like wattle and daub (Link to Art QCA Unit 4c.
◆ Make designs for Celtic cloth. (Link to Art QCA Unit 3b)
◆ Make woven Celtic patterns using paper strips. (Link to Art QCA Unit 3b)
◆ Cook and taste porridge.

Literacy

Page 18	Page 19
visual report	visual report

◆ In pairs, pupils discuss the labelled picture on pp 18–19 and use the information to create a skeleton notes for a visual report. Use the skeleton notes to write a report about the different aspects of a Celtic farm.
◆ The information could also be used to create a recount skeleton to describe the events in a farmers' day. Pupils then use skeleton notes to create a series of freeze frames to recount the farmer's day.

History

Key concepts
◆ To use the terms 'invade' and 'settle'.
◆ To place the Celtic and Roman periods in a chronological framework.

Key vocabulary
◆ *invade, settle, conquer, Caesar, enemies*

Suggested activities
◆ Identify key dates in Caesar's life and place on the class timeline.
◆ Discuss with pupils other events that were taking place at the same time e.g. *100 BC Caesar's birth, the Celts were settled in Britain and were living without further invasion. 44 BC Caesar died and AD 60 Britain invaded again.*
◆ Pupils take statements and dates about Caesar's life and organize them into a chronological timeline of Caesar's life.

Literacy

page 20	page 21
written recount	written recount

◆ In pairs, pupils use these pages to make skeleton notes to recount the life of Julius Caesar.
◆ Pupils retell Caesar's life using the skeleton notes in a variety of ways e.g. in the first person, as a news reporter talking about the death of Caesar.
◆ Write a newspaper report on Caesar's death that recounts his life. Remind pupils of the need for a heading, and an introductory paragraph with a leading sentence.
◆ If you are using these pages with an older class, use these pages to secure understanding of biographical recounts. Point out: use of adjectives; paragraphs show chronological order; use of quotation.

History

Key concepts

- Use terms 'invade' and 'settle'.
- To place the Celtic and Roman periods on a chronological framework.

Key vocabulary

- *invade, settle, invasion, conquest, capture*

Suggested activities

- Give pupils cards containing dates and captions. In pairs, pupils sequence the dates so they are in chronological order.
- Place key dates on the class timeline.
- Pupils use role play, as reporters, to show key events: e.g. *the conquest of Britain; building Hadrian's Wall; the Romans leaving Britain.*
- Explore the Romans departure from the point of view of a number of characters: e.g. *soldier, a Governor with a Celtic wife and family, a Celtic family living and working as slaves to a Roman family.* Discuss how this would affect their lives.

Literacy

page 22	page 23
┼┼┼→	┼┼┼→
visual recount	visual recount

- Use the visual recount on these pages to identify the key points in the invasion. Ask pupils to decide the three most important dates and events in the invasion and create an oral comic strip presentation.
- In pairs, pupils discuss the information to create skeleton notes for a recount of the invasion.
- Pupils could use skeleton notes to write a series of letters/diary entries as if written by a Roman soldier who was part of the invasion and who settled in Britain.

History

Key concepts

- To know the main events in Boudicca's revolt.
- To understand the reason for the revolt.

Key vocabulary

- *Boudicca, Iceni tribe, chariot, Colchester, St Albans*

Suggested activities

- Place events of Iceni tribe's revolt on the class timeline.
- Through drama, pupils create a series of freeze frames that recount the events of Boudicca's revolt. Pupils express feelings of different characters. (Links to Drama and PHSE/Citizenship)
- In pairs or groups, pupils brainstorm a list of reasons why Boudicca and the Iceni felt that it would be better to live without Roman help. Then repeat for the Roman point of view.
- In groups, use role play to show a meeting between the Iceni and the Romans where various viewpoints are discussed.
- Search different sources (see Bibliography) that have accounts of Boudicca's revolt and identify similarities and differences in the reporting.

Literacy

page 24	page 25
┼┼┼→	┼┼┼→
visual recount	visual recount

These pages are used as part of the featured example to teach pupils how to read and write **recount** texts. See pp 42–47 of these teacher's notes

- In pairs, pupils discuss the information on pp 23–24 and create their own recount skeleton notes about the events of Boudicca's revolt.

History

Key concepts

◆ To understand that there are different opinions about Boudicca.

◆ To understand that there are different interpretations of the revolt.

Key vocabulary

◆ *Boudicca, revolt, Iceni, Celtic chief, tribes*

Suggested activities

◆ Use pp 26–27 to identify differing viewpoints of the revolt. Orally, in pairs, pupils expand on reasons given.

◆ Stage a 'mock trial' where different characters come forward with evidence for and against Boudicca. Ask the class come to decide whether she should have revolted or not. (Links to Drama and PHSE/ Citizenship)

◆ Search other sources (see Bibliography) that recount the events of Boudicca's revolt to identify a) further details, b) opinions of the revolt.

Literacy

page 26	page 27
✳✳ ✳✳ ✳✳	✳✳ ✳✳ ✳✳
visual discussion	visual discussion

◆ Use these pages to support speaking and listening. When giving evidence during the mock trial, encourage pupils to state their opinion initially and then elaborate on it. E.g. *My husband died in the revolt. He died needlessly,* (opinion). *This means that I have to find work and feed my family as well as do the tasks that he did. We should* **all** *have lived side by side with the Romans as we had done before. Now the Romans watch us all the time and treat us differently to the way they did before.* (Elaboration)

◆ In Y4–6/P5–7 pupils could create a discussion skeleton by writing notes under headings 'for' and 'against', relating to each of the frames on these pages.

◆ The skeleton notes could then be used to write a full discussion about the benefits and drawbacks of Boudicca's actions.

History

Key concept

◆ To know that there is evidence that tells about life in Roman Britain.

Key vocabulary

◆ *evidence, historic site, artefact, archaeological evidence*

Suggested activities

◆ Visit a Roman site and collect evidence of Roman life using a digital camera.

◆ Using additional resources, create pictures and captions that explain what the remains might have been like originally.

◆ Use other sources (see Bibliography) to locate other Roman remains around Britain and locate on a map.

◆ Create a guide to Roman Britain to show others where to find the best remains of Roman roads, baths, mosaics, defences, villas etc.

◆ Meet an archaeologist to discuss how they know when they have found a site and how they excavate objects.

Literacy

page 28	page 29
visual report	visual report

In pairs, pupils discuss the visual report on pp 28–29 to create skeleton notes for a report about one Roman site in Britain.

◆ Pupils use further sources (see bibliography) and write a full report using ICT, downloading and inserting a picture of their particular site into the text. (Link to ICT.)

◆ Use these pages also to identify the way information is presented e.g. headings, captions, bullet lists etc.

◆ Point out that the sites are listed alphabetically and use to reinforce pupils' knowledge of the purpose and structure of reference texts. Compare to other guides e.g. Visitor's guides, CD-ROMs etc. Discuss other ways this information could have been organized and presented.

History

Key concepts

◆ To understand about aspects of life in Roman Britain.

◆ To make comparisons between Celtic and Roman lifestyles.

Key vocabulary

◆ *villa, slave, bath house, hypocaust*

Suggested activities

Use these pages as a starting point for research about Roman villas.

Use further sources (see Bibliography) to find out about the inside of a villa.

◆ In pairs, pupils read and research for information to construct a floor plan of a villa.

◆ As a class make an annotated diagram of a villa using pupils' research information.

◆ Pupils make comparisons between a Roman villa and a Celtic farm. Use a comparison grid to support pupils.

◆ Pupils use role play to show different behaviour of slave and master, using evidence from research to support their roles. (Link to Drama.)

◆ Design and make a mosaic (Link to Art QCA Unit 3b.)

◆ Pupils use an atlas to locate sites of Roman villas shown on map. (Link to Geography.)

◆ With support, pupils search for web sites giving more information about Roman villas in Britain. (Link to ICT.)

Literacy

Page 30	Page 31
┼┼┼─➤	⌀
written recount	visual report

P 30 is used as a featured example to teach pupils how to read and write **recount** texts. See pp 42–47 of these teacher's notes.

History

Key concept

◆ To understand about evidence that tells us about life in Roman Britain.

Key vocabulary

◆ *engineer, inventions, surveyor, foundations, layers*

Suggested activities

◆ Pupils skim pages to identify why the Romans decided they needed to build such well-made roads everywhere they went. Ensure pupils reference their answers.

◆ For a classroom display, create an annotated diagram of a Roman road with accurate proportions. (Link to DT.)

◆ Create a mini Roman road by following the information given on pp 32–33 outside in school grounds. (Link to DT.)

◆ Locate Roman roads in Britain on a map. (Link to Geography.)

◆ Pupils research other great Roman inventions and create a 'Did you know?' quiz.

Literacy

Page 32	Page 33
⌀➤⌀➤	⌀➤⌀➤
visual explanation	visual explanation

These pages are used as a featured example to teach pupils how to read and write **explanation** texts. See pp 30–35 of these teacher's notes

In addition:

◆ Use these pages to create a set of written instructions on how to build a Roman road.

◆ In pairs, pupils discuss the visual explanation on pp 32–33 and create skeleton notes for written instructions. Pupils then use their notes to write up a set of instructions using the textual features described on p 38 of these teacher's notes.

History

Key concepts
◆ To identify evidence about life in Roman Britain.
◆ Answer and ask questions about what survived from Roman settlement.

Key vocabulary
◆ *bath house, furnace, flue*

Suggested activities
◆ Use illustration on p 35 to help pupils to role play a visit to the bath house. Pupils take roles as slaves, masseurs and clients. Encourage them to re-enact the routine in different parts of the bath house.
◆ Demonstrate how hot air rises. (Link to Science QCA Unit 4d.)
◆ Pupils write a first person recount of a visit by a Roman to the bath house, based on information on these pages.

Literacy

Page 34	Page 35
○→⟡→⟡	○→⟡→⟡
written explanation	visual explanation

These pages are used as featured examples to teach pupils how to read and write **explanation** texts. See pp 30–35 of these teacher's notes.

History

Key concept
◆ To learn about aspects of life in Roman Britain.

Key vocabulary
◆ *board game, dice, counter*

Suggested activities
◆ In pairs, pupils make board game, making accurate measurements. (Links to Maths and DT.)
◆ Research other games that the Romans played using further sources (see Bibliography).
◆ Compare and contrast the types of games played by the Romans with those played today.
◆ Pupils summarize what they know about aspects of Roman life under the following headings: *home, jobs, free time, food, religion* and compare with either Celtic life, or present-day life. This could be presented on a class grid structure as a comparative report (see p 26 of these notes).

Literacy

Page 36	Page 37
○→○→○→	○→○→○→
visual instructions	visual instructions

◆ These pages are used as a featured example to teach pupils how to read and write **instruction** texts. See pp 36–41 of these teacher's notes.

History

Key concepts

◆ To learn about aspects of life in Roman and Celtic Britain.

◆ To know evidence that tells us about life in Roman Britain.

Key vocabulary

◆ *temple, god, goddess, mosaic, curse, worship, tombstone, spirit*

Suggested activities

◆ Use these pages and further sources (see Bibliography) to find out about other Celtic and Roman gods and goddesses.

◆ As a class, compare Roman and Celtic temples and tombs with places of worship and burial that pupils have seen or visited. (Link to RE.)

◆ Design and make a mosaic of a Roman or Celtic god or goddess. (Link to DT.)

Literacy

page 38	page 39
written comparative report	written comparative report

◆ These pages are used as a featured example to teach pupils how to read and write **comparative report** texts. See pp 24–29 of these teacher's notes.

History

Key concepts

◆ To understand about aspects of life in Roman and Celtic Britain.

◆ To know evidence that tells us about life in Roman Britain.

Key vocabulary

◆ *society, multi-cultural, customs, settlers*

Suggested activities

◆ In pairs, pupils create fact files itemising '*What the Romans have done for us*' using information on these pages and others.

◆ Pupils use evidence from these pages to create the people identified and their histories, then use role play to interview each other while playing these characters.

◆ Pupils look at own family trees to find out nationalities and locate where their families originate from. (Link to Citizenship QCA Unit 5.)

Literacy

page 40	page 41
written comparative report	written comparative report

Use these pages to identify the main points of a report text.

◆ Using OHP, demonstrate how to text mark to identify aspects of Celtic and Roman life.

◆ Pupils record information on a grid to create a comparative report.

◆ Encourage pupils to scan for information about specific people in the text.

◆ In pairs, pupils use whiteboards to make skeleton notes on aspects of the text, and discuss how they made their notes with teacher. Erase any unnecessary words.

◆ Demonstrate how to make a visual version of the text by using a report skeleton.

◆ Remind pupils that reports move from general terms to specific (see p 26 of these teacher's notes).

Older pupils could use the section on Latin words for a discussion on the origin of words and place names.

History

Key concepts
◆ To understand about aspects of life in Roman and Celtic Britain.
◆ To know evidence that tells us about life in Roman Britain.

Key vocabulary
◆ *multi-cultural, tax, settlers, retirement, barracks, fort*

Suggested activities
◆ Ask pairs/groups of pupils to give reasons why Roman rule was good and use other pages in the pupils' book to provide evidence to support their point of view. Encourage pupils to explain their opinions using '*We/ I think this because…*'. Repeat for the Celtic point of view.
◆ Hold a class debate with half the class on the side on the Romans the other on the Celts' side.

Literacy

Page 42	Page 43
✳✳ ✳✳ ✳✳	✳✳ ✳✳ ✳✳
written discussion	written discussion

Use these pages on an OHP to revisit text marking and note-making, demonstrating how to identify key words in a sentence.

◆ Start with the main reason Roman rule was good i.e. *They civilized the Celts.* Ask pupils to find evidence in the first paragraph that shows why the Celts needed to become civilized e.g. *No baths.* Record on a class grid.
◆ In pairs, pupils read second paragraph to find other 'civilized' Roman ways the Celts had yet to learn e.g. *use of coins.* Discuss the key words they select and their reasons for choosing them. If suitable, add to class grid. Repeat for the rest of the text.
◆ Using p 43, pupils make skeleton notes on the opposing argument which suggests reasons why Roman rule was bad for the Celts e.g. *Lack of respect for the Celts' bravery, craft skills and folk-lore.*

History

Key concept
◆ Recognize the reasons some people have moved away are the same as people's reasons today.

Key vocabulary
◆ *settlement, emigration, refugee*

Suggested activities
◆ As a class, review the timeline on pp 8–9 in the pupils' book to put the Romans' departure from Britain in context.
◆ Discuss with pupils their own family trees to identify where people where born. Discuss reasons why people have moved from where they were born e.g. *new job, to be closer to family, war, disruption and other factors.* (Link to Citizenship.)
◆ Locate information about where pupils come from on a map. Relate to where different members of families live. (Link to Geography.)

Literacy

Page 44	Page 45
○→☼→☽	○→☼→☽
written explanation	written explanation

◆ In pairs, pupils discuss the written historical explanation on pp 44–45 and identify the series of events that led to the Romans leaving Britain.
◆ Support pupils in making effective notes by modelling how to identify key words or phrases in a sentence.
◆ Record key events and dates on cards. In pairs, pupils use the cards and events to orally explain why the Romans left Britain.
◆ Demonstrate how to make a visual explanation skeleton about *Why the Romans left Britain* creating a flow chart covering the main events i.e. *using the paragraph headings.*
◆ In pairs, pupils return to the written explanation and together create their own, more detailed flow charts to explain the Romans' departure from Britain.

History

Key concept

◆ To use vocabulary associated with the Romans.

Suggested activities

Use this page to search for the meanings of key vocabulary to further pupils' understanding of different aspects of the Romans. Identify word from reading that are unknown and use the **glossary** to further understanding and to clarify information learnt.

Literacy

Use this page to locate information confidently and efficiently through using the glossary.

◆ Remind pupils of the purpose of a glossary: to explain to the reader the meaning of words or terms that are specific to the subject of the text.

◆ Using some of the key words identified both in the pupils' book and in these notes, show how to scan the glossary to find some of the meanings. Point out that the words are in alphabetical order rather than in subject order.

History

Key concepts

◆ Use the **bibliography** to find further information on the topic.
◆ Use index to locate information in different parts of the book.

Literacy

Use these pages to teach the pupils the purpose and function of a bibliography.

Point out to pupils that this bibliography:

◆ provides a reference point for further reading;
◆ is organized alphabetically using the surname of the author;
◆ provides the ISBN number (International Standard Book Number) as well as the title of the reference;
◆ contains some of the following sources: books, websites, articles, periodicals or journals.

Discuss how different source material (i.e. books, websites, CD-ROMs etc.) are organized, e.g. *alphabetic, thematic, chronological.* Compare details provided in *Roman Britain* with material found in a different source.

Use the **index** to find specific information. Point out the following:

◆ At times, it is quicker to use an index rather than using the contents.
◆ An index sometimes doesn't take you to the information you want – you may have to go to a number of pages.
◆ *Skimming* is a more general approach than *scanning.* Both skills can be used to obtain information quickly but have different purposes, for example, scanning when you want to know something specific and skimming if you want a general overview before obtaining details or making a close read.

Teaching pupils how to read and write report text

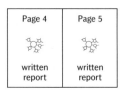

Page 4	Page 5
written report	written report

Reading a report text

Read pp 4–5 of *Roman Britain* with the pupils. You will need:

◆ The report text on pp 4–5 (the text-only version on p 21 of these notes can be enlarged/photocopied/made into an OHT for annotation);
◆ p 20 of these notes which can be enlarged/photocopied/made into OHT for annotation.

Audience and purpose

SHARED READING ACTIVITY

Talk about how the intended audience and purpose affects the language and layout.

Audience – adults/pupils who want to know information about Roman Britain.

Purpose – to give factual information about Roman Britain.

Content and organization

SHARED WRITING ACTIVITY

Show pupils how the content of this written report is organized by demonstrating its content as a report skeleton (see p 23 of these notes). Identify key words and phrases in the text that indicate the subject of the paragraph. Point out that headings provide a clue to the main subject matter of the paragraph and that paragraphs are non-chronological and could be written in any order since they just describe different aspects of the Roman Empire. Differing aspects of Roman life are referred to, e.g. *cities, people, empire*. The pages serve as an introduction to the Romans and deal with information in general terms.

Language features and style

SHARED READING ACTIVITY

Return to the written report and talk about the way language has been used to achieve the effects the author intended (see annotated version on p 22 of these notes). Point out the use of the past tense, because this is a historical report (remind pupils that reports are often written in the present tense). Specific dates and details are given e.g. 2000 years ago, AD 300. Headings indicate new aspect being introduced, e.g. *Splendid city, Roman people*, and paragraphs move from general to specific, as in section on 'Roman remains'. Specific vocabulary is used for clarity, e.g. *insulae, aqueducts* and explanations and definitions, to ensure understanding on the part of the reader e.g. *'insulae' which means 'islands'*.

Identify information that pupils would like to find out about the Romans and suggest possible sources of information.

INDEPENDENT ACTIVITY

Using further sources, work in groups to add further notes about one aspect of Roman life identified in this report, e.g. *Roman army*.

Page 10	Page 11
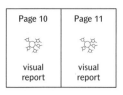 visual report	visual report

Writing a report text

Use pp 10–11 of *Roman Britain* as a basis for pupils' own written reports. You will need:

◆ the visual report on pp 10–11;
◆ p 20 of these notes enlarged/photocopied/made into an OHT for annotation.

Content and organization

SHARED READING ACTIVITY

Revise the content and organization of the report from the previous session (see p 23 of these notes).

Tell pupils that they are going to write a leaflet for young Romans about life in the Roman army.

PAIRED READING AND WRITING ACTIVITY

Pairs of pupils discuss the notes shown in the visual report on pp 10–11 and turn them into a report skeleton about the Roman army. Ask them to add any additional information they already know to the skeleton if they think it will be relevant to their intended audience.

Language features and style

Remind pupils of the language features and style of report texts (see p 20 of these notes).

Audience and purpose

SHARED WRITING ACTIVITY

Discuss the audience (young Romans who know nothing about the Roman army but are considering joining up), and purpose (to give clear information about what they can expect as a Roman soldier).

Suggest how they might start the leaflet by writing an introductory paragraph on a general theme, for example:
The Roman army is a world-beating army. It has helped to make the Roman Empire as large as it is today. Read this leaflet and find out why every young Roman wants to be part of it.

Demonstrate how they could continue by using a question:
Why become a soldier?
Young Romans who join the army volunteer because they know that it is a world-beating force and they want to be part of it. After all, the Roman Empire is the greatest in the world!

Discuss the following points with pupils:

◆ how the question works as a heading, drawing the reader in, and then look at how the paragraph tries to answer the question;
◆ the use of the present tense – because they are writing as if they were 'in role'.

Use paired talk and supported composition to scribe together the next paragraph, answering the following question:

What training and equipment do Roman soldiers get?

Remind pupils that the text is aimed at a general audience so there are no personal references.

INDEPENDENT WRITING ACTIVITY

Pupils write up their report independently, using a series of questions as a 'scaffold' for each paragraph, to give it structure.

About report text

Audience and purpose

Audience – someone who wants to know about the topic.

Purpose – to describe what something is like.

> Sometimes you may know more about the age or interests of your reader

Content and organization

- **non-chronological** information
- **introductory sentence or paragraph** says what the report is going to be about
- the information is sorted into groups or **categories**
- reports may include short pieces of explanation

> This means it ISN'T written in time order, like a story or recount

> What something looks like, where it is found . . .

Language features

- written in the **present tense**
- usually **general nouns and pronouns** (not particular people or things)
- **factual descriptive words**, not like the descriptions in a story
- words and devices that show **comparison and contrast**
- **third person** writing to make the report **impersonal and formal**
- **technical words and phrases** – which you may need to explain to the reader
- use of **examples** to help the reader understand the technical words

> Past tense may be used in historical material

> You would write about dogs in general, not a particular dog

> You would say powerful beams, not beautiful bright beams

> Expressions like have in common, the same as . . ., on the other hand, however. . .

> Unusual words that go with the topic such as, canine, translucent and wingspan

> Wingspan is the distance between the tips of a bird's outstretched wings

The basic skeleton for making notes is a spidergram

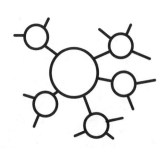

An example of a report text

What do we know about the Romans?

The Romans lived in Italy over 2000 years ago. At first, they were farmers. But then they fought against other people in Italy, and took over their lands. This made them rich and very powerful.

Splendid city

The Romans turned their home town, Rome, into a splendid city. It had palaces and temples, sports arenas, shopping malls, take-away food shops, schools, libraries, public baths and lavatories, and the first-ever blocks of flats. (The Romans called them 'insulae', which means 'islands', because each block was a separate community.) Rome was also the centre of a huge network of well-made roads.

Roman people

The city of Rome grew very quickly. Many different people lived there – rich nobles and businessmen, ordinary workers and slaves. By AD 300, a million people lived in Rome. It was the largest city in the world.

Roman remains

The remains of many ancient Roman buildings still survive today. They show us what life was like in Roman times. Vast underground drains, long bridges and tall aqueducts tell us about Roman engineering methods.

Army and empire

The Roman army was the best in the world. Roman soldiers marched out of Italy and conquered lands in Europe, North Africa, and the Middle East. They conquered most of Britain, too. The conquered lands were called the Roman empire. Everyone living in the empire had to pay Roman taxes and obey Roman laws. To keep control, Roman soldiers lived in camps and forts all over the empire. They guarded frontiers and tried to stop conquered peoples rebelling against Roman rule. But after many centuries, there were more and more attacks, and the Roman empire was destroyed.

Language features and style of report text

What do we know about the Romans?

The Romans lived in Italy over 2000 years ago. At first, they were farmers. But then they fought against other people in Italy, and took over their lands. This made them rich and very powerful.

Splendid city

The Romans turned their home town, Rome, into a splendid city. It had palaces and temples, sports arenas, shopping malls, take-away food shops, schools, libraries, public baths and lavatories, and the first-ever blocks of flats. (The Romans called them 'insulae', which means 'islands', because each block was a separate community.) Rome was also the centre of a huge network of well-made roads.

Roman people

The city of Rome grew very quickly. Many different people lived there – rich nobles and businessmen, ordinary workers and slaves. By AD 300, a million people lived in Rome. It was the largest city in the world.

Roman remains

The remains of many ancient Roman buildings still survive today. They show us what life was like in Roman times. Vast underground drains, long bridges and tall aqueducts tell us about Roman engineering methods.

Army and empire

The Roman army was the best in the world. Roman soldiers marched out of Italy and conquered lands in Europe, North Africa, and the Middle East. They conquered most of Britain, too. The conquered lands were called the Roman empire. Everyone living in the empire had to pay Roman taxes and obey Roman laws. To keep control, Roman soldiers lived in camps and forts all over the empire. They guarded frontiers and tried to stop conquered peoples rebelling against Roman rule. But after many centuries, there were more and more attacks, and the Roman empire was destroyed.

Annotations (margin notes):

- Past tense as the subject matter is historical
- Heading indicating aspect of Romans to be described (categories)
- Simple sentence to maintain clarity of information for the reader
- Technical vocabulary relating to Roman culture to give details to reader
- Past tense throughout (as this is historical)
- General nouns throughout e.g. **lands**
- Style formal, factual
- Third person
- Non-chronological
- Phrases added to explain terms to reader and ensure understanding
- Specific amounts to give accurate detail
- Non-chronological information

If you are using this text with other year groups, then also highlight these features:

Y4/P5 ◆ How reports are divided up into sections by sub-headings that indicate to the reader what the content will be
◆ The use of noun phrases to give factual detail e.g. **rich and very powerful, vast underground drains, long bridges and tall aqueducts**

Y5/P6 ◆ Focus on how to move on ideas within a paragraph from general information to specific detail with the use of three or four sentences
◆ Develop use of technical vocabulary to give clarity and specific information e.g **taxes**

Y6/P7 ◆ Secure the use of impersonal language in report writing, e.g. **this is known as**
◆ Create a bank of impersonal phrases that are used in reports e.g. **for example**
◆ Focus on distinguishing between active and passive in report writing

Content and organization of the report text

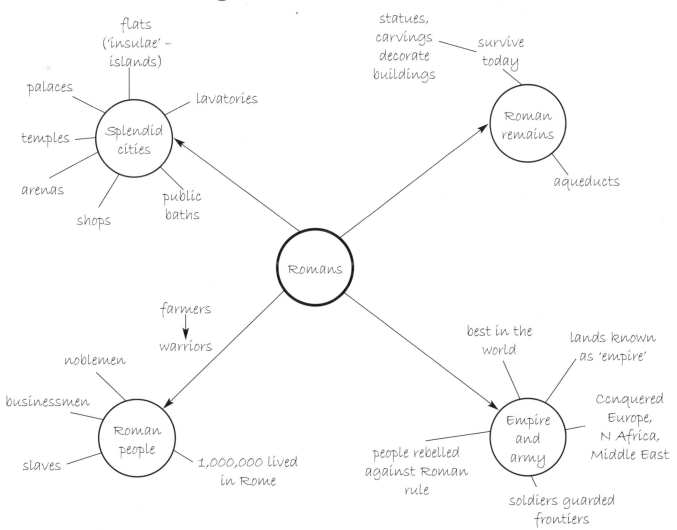

Teaching pupils how to read and write a comparative report text

Page 38	Page 39
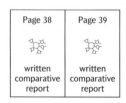	
written comparative report	written comparative report

Reading a comparative report text

Read pp 38–39 of *Roman Britain* with the pupils. You will need:

- The comparative report text on pp 38–39 (The text-only version on p 27 of these notes can be enlarged/photocopied/made into an OHT for annotation);
- p 26 of these notes which can be enlarged/photocopied/made into OHT for annotation.

Audience and purpose

Define comparative report text as a text that compares two things that have some similar and some different features. Discuss how the intended audience and purpose affects the language and layout.

> SHARED READING ACTIVITY

Audience – adults/ pupils who want to know the similarities and differences between the way Romans and the Celts worshipped.

Purpose – to show the similarities and differences between Roman and Celtic religious practices.

Content and organization

> SHARED WRITING ACTIVITY

Show pupils how the content of this written comparative report is organized by showing its content as a comparative report skeleton (see p 29 of these notes). Point out that each paragraph refers to a different aspect of Roman and Celtic religious beliefs and that paragraphs highlight similarities as well as differences between them.

Headings indicate the subject matter of each paragraph and the first sentence in the introductory paragraph gives general details while the second sentence moves to specifics.

Language features and style

> SHARED READING ACTIVITY

Return to the text and talk about the way language has been used to achieve the effects the author intended (see annotated version on p 28 of these notes). Point out that past tense is used because it is a historical report. Connectives such as *'also'*, *'as well'*, *'too'*, are used to signal similarities. Specific places and names are used to give clarity and detail to the report e.g. *Lug, Jupiter*. Additional phrases are added to sentences e.g. *Epona, goddess of horses*. Examples are given to ensure reader's understanding e.g. *'for example, as a human, an animal or a bird*.

> INDEPENDENT ACTIVITY

Ask pupils to compare an aspect of Roman life with life now, such as: *school in Roman times, Roman houses*.

In a plenary session, pupils can practise speaking and listening skills by making oral comparisons, focusing on using comparative language.

Writing a comparative report text

Use pp 12–13 of *Roman Britain* as a basis for pupils' own comparative report. You will need:

◆ the visual comparative report on pp 12–13;

◆ p 26 of these notes enlarged/photocopied/made into an OHT for annotation.

Content and organization

> **SHARED READING ACTIVITY**

Revise the content and organization of the written comparative report from the previous session (see p 29 of these notes).

> **PAIRED READING AND WRITING ACTIVITY**

In pairs, pupils discuss the visual report on pp 12–13 of the pupils' book to create a skeleton comparative report. As a class, discuss possible headings for paragraphs e.g. *clothes*, *weapons* and *armour*. This could be done on a chart or table with two columns, one for Romans, one for Celts, and a different paragraph heading for each row.

Remind pupils to look for details and to text mark key words and phrases, prior to writing notes or completing their charts.

Language features and style

Remind pupils of the language features of comparative report text (see p 26 of these notes).

Audience and purpose

Discuss the audience for pupils' writing (adults/pupils who want to know what similarities and differences there are between Roman and Celtic soldiers) and purpose (to inform readers of similarities and differences between Roman and Celtic soldiers).

> **SHARED WRITING ACTIVITY**

Demonstrate by writing a short introductory paragraph indicating to the reader the subject matter.

Both the Romans and the Celts had armies of fierce soldiers. Both trained hard, but what were the differences between them?

Follow this by showing the pupils how to make comparisons within a paragraph.

What did Roman and Celtic soldiers look like?

Most Celtic warriors were very tall and strong with either red or blonde hair brushed back like a horse's mane. They had long moustaches and wore body paint called woad on their faces when they went to war. Most Roman soldiers, however, were about medium height and usually had dark eyes and dark hair. Unlike the Celtic warriors, Roman soldiers were always shaved and often suntanned.

Ask pupils to point out the connecting devices used to indicate differences e.g. *however, unlike*.

Discuss how you have included a lot of information within sentences by using different conjunctions e.g. *with, and, when*.

> **INDEPENDENT WRITING ACTIVITY**

Pupils write up the remaining paragraphs about *What clothes did they wear?* and *What weapons and armour did they use?* working independently.

About comparative report text

Audience and purpose

Audience – someone who wants to know the similarities and differences between items with a common element.

Purpose – to identify what the similarities and differences are.

> I want to know what's the difference between these two computers

Content and organization

- **non-chronological** information

> This means that it is NOT written in time order, like a story or a recount

- **introductory sentence or paragraph** saying what the report is going to be about, including an indication that it is going to identify similarities and differences e.g *Many parts are the same, but there are some that are different*
- the information is sorted into groups or **categories** – each paragraph focuses on what is the same and what is different
- reports may include short pieces of **explanation**

> Both evergreen and deciduous trees have bark. Bark on deciduous trees is . . . while bark on evergreen trees is. . .

Language features

- written in the **present tense** unless historical, when it is written in the **past**
- usually **general nouns and pronouns** (not particular people or things)
- **factual descriptive words**, not like descriptions in a story

> You would say powerful beams, not beautiful, bright beams

> You would write about dogs in general, not a particular dog

- connectives that indicate a relationship between ideas. Some indicating **comparison and contrast** e.g *as well as, too, but they also, sometimes, most, both have, great deal in common*
- **third person** writing to make the report **impersonal and formal**
- **technical words and phrases** that need to be explained to the reader
- use of **examples** to help the reader understand the technical words

> Wingspan is the distance between the tips of a bird's outstretched wings

> Unusual words that link to the topic such as canine, translucent usually explained using the connective: 'This means. . .'

An example of a comparative report text

Temples and tombs

At home in Rome, the Romans worshipped many different gods and goddesses. Jupiter was the most important. He protected the Roman state.

Celtic people also honoured many gods, such as Lug, god of music, and Epona, goddess of horses. They said prayers and gave offerings to holy mountains, rivers and trees. When the Romans came to Britain, they started to worship Celtic gods and goddesses, as well as their own. Sometimes, they joined Roman and Celtic gods together, or gave Celtic gods Roman names.

Homes for the gods

In Britain, the Romans built huge temples for gods and goddesses to live in, just like those they built in Rome. They carved lifelike statues of gods, and pictured them in mosaics and wall-paintings. The Celts made statues of their gods, too. They preferred to worship in the open air.

Remembering the dead

The Romans believed that the spirits of dead people went on living for as long as their families and friends remembered them. So they paid for tombstones, with carved portraits of dead people, to stand close to their graves. The Celts believed that people's spirits lived on after death, and that they might be born again, for example, as a human, an animal or a bird.

Language features and style of the comparative report text

Side annotations (left):

- Past tense throughout (as this is historical)
- General nouns throughout to name similar things e.g. **gods**
- Specific nouns to describe different people or things e.g. **Jupiter, Lug**
- Style formal, factual
- Third person
- Connectives used to refer to comparisons/differences e.g. **also**
- Non-chronological

Technical vocabulary used relating to subject matter to ensure clarity of meaning

Heading indicating the subject matter of the paragraph

Connective signalling consequence of beliefs highlighted in the previous sentence

Side annotations (right):

Past tense because it is an historical report

Names adding specific detail

Specific places mentioned

Connectives used to highlight how Romans and Celts became similar

Example provided to add explanation and ensure readers' understanding

Temples and tombs

At home in Rome, the Romans worshipped many different gods and goddesses. Jupiter was the most important. He protected the Roman state.

Celtic people also honoured many gods, such as Lug, god of music, and Epona, goddess of horses. They said prayers and gave offerings to holy mountains, rivers and trees. When the Romans came to Britain, they started to worship Celtic gods and goddesses, as well as their own. Sometimes, they joined Roman and Celtic gods together, or gave Celtic gods Roman names.

Homes for the gods

In Britain, the Romans built huge temples for gods and goddesses to live in, just like those they built in Rome. They carved lifelike statues of gods, and pictured them in mosaics and wall-paintings. The Celts made statues of their gods, too. They preferred to worship their gods in the open air.

Remembering the dead

The Romans believed that the spirits of dead people went on living for as long as their families and friends remembered them. So they paid for tombstones, with carved portraits of dead people, to stand close to their graves. The Celts believed that people's spirits lived on after death, and that they might be born again, for example, as a human, an animal or a bird.

If you are using this text for other year groups, then also highlight these features:

Y4 /P5 ◆ Support children with making simple comparative notes by using simple grids that compare and contrast simple features

Y5/P6 ◆ Focus on the structure and organization of comparative reports. Identify how they differ in language features from other reports
◆ Develop a bank of words, phrases and clauses that enable writers to compare and contrast e.g. **both contain, although, however, the snail differs from the slug because...**

Y6/P7 ◆ Secure the use of impersonal language in report writing e.g. **this is known as**
◆ Create a bank of impersonal phrases that are used in reports e.g. **for example**
◆ Focus on distinguishing between active and passive in report writing

Content and organization of the comparative report text

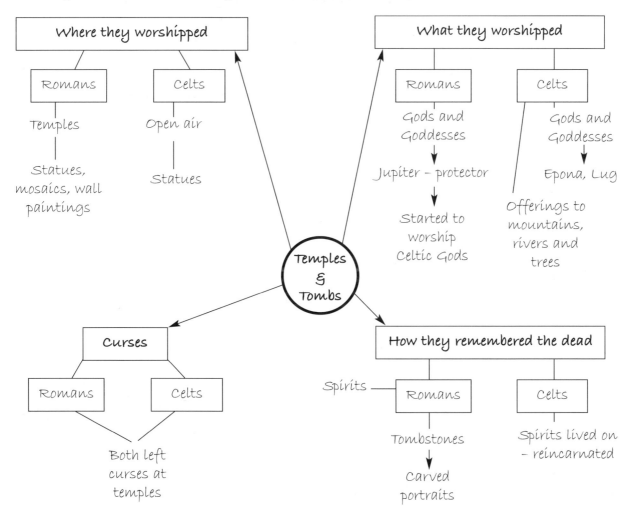

Teaching pupils how to read and write an explanation text

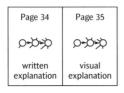

Page 34	Page 35
written explanation	visual explanation

Reading an explanation text

Read pp 34–35 of *Roman Britain* with the pupils. You will need:

◆ the explanation text on p 34 (the text-only version on p 33 of these notes can be enlarged/ photocopied/ made into an OHT for annotation);

◆ p 32 of these notes which can be enlarged/photocopied/ made into an OHT for annotation.

Audience and purpose

> SHARED
> READING
> ACTIVITY

Talk about how the audience and purpose affects the language and layout.

Audience – people who do not understand how Roman baths were heated.

Purpose – to explain in simple steps how Roman baths were heated.

Content and organization

> SHARED
> WRITING
> ACTIVITY

Show pupils how the content of this explanation text is organized by showing its content as an explanation skeleton (see p 35 of these notes). Point out that the question that tells the reader what is to be explained and sub-headings help the reader understand the process in small steps. The small circular diagram inset on the bigger picture helps to explain the bathing routine visually.

Language features and style

> SHARED
> READING
> ACTIVITY

Return to the text and talk about the way language has been used to achieve the effects the author intended (see annotated version on p 34 of these notes). Point out the 'How' question which suggest that an explanation will be given. Technical vocabulary: *hypocaust, furnace, flues, central heating,* is used to ensure precision; simple sentences help maintain clarity. Notice the cause and effect connectives within complex sentences e.g. *As the fire burned, flues pulled. When the water in the tank became warm, it rose.*

> INDEPENDENT
> WRITING
> ACTIVITY

Pupils create an explanation skeleton by making notes into a flow chart to explain the heating process in the bath house. They can use the cutaway diagram on p 35 of *Roman Britain* to help them understand the process more clearly.

Page 32

○→☆→○

visual explanation

Page 33

○→☆→○

visual explanation

Writing an explanation text

Use pp 32–33 of *Roman Britain* as a basis for pupils' own explanation texts. You will need:

◆ the visual explanation on pp 32–33;
◆ p 32 of these notes enlarged/photocopied/made into an OHT for annotation.

SHARED
READING
ACTIVITY

PAIRED
READING AND
WRITING ACIVITY

Content and organization

Revise the content and organization of the explanation text from the previous session (see p 35 of these notes).

In pairs, pupils discuss the visual explanation on pp 32–33 of the pupils' book and make notes for an explanation skeleton. Remind pupils that an explanation skeleton should be a flow chart, following the numbered panels. Discuss each step in the road-building process and work out its function.

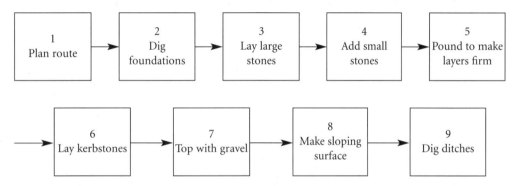

Language features and style

Remind pupils of the language features of explanation texts (see p 32 of these notes).

Audience and purpose

SHARED
WRITING
ACTIVITY

Discuss the audience for the pupils' written explanation text (readers who nothing about the way Roman roads were built) and the purpose (to explain how the Romans built roads that have lasted a very long time).

Demonstrate writing the first part of the explanation (imitating some of the language features of the written explanation on p 34 of the pupils' book) e.g.

Why did Roman roads last so long?
Roman roads lasted for thousands of years because they were so well built. Some are still used because they follow the best, straight route.

How did they make them so well?
Firstly, the Romans looked for the best route for the road to take, then they cleared the site so there was enough space to build a good, wide road. Then they dug really deep foundations which were more than 30 cm deep. This meant that the new road would stay firm and last for a long time, like a well-built house.

The foundations were filled in with large, strong stones to give the road a good solid base, then smaller stones were put on top of the large ones. Next, they pounded the stones with something heavy, such as big logs, because they needed to make the small stones pack down between the larger stones. The Romans did this so that the road would not be ground down or churned up into mud when people travelled over it...

Discuss with pupils how the paragraphs use the information and give a logical reason for why the Romans did certain things when they built their roads.

Comment also on the use of connectives: *because, so, then, next, such as, so that* etc.

Remind pupils to re-read their paragraph to make sure they have answered the question.

INDEPENDENT
WRITING
ACTIVITY

Pupils write their own version of the first paragraph of the explanation and then explain the rest of the road-building process.

About explanation text

Audience and purpose

Audience – someone who wants to understand the process (how or why it happens).

Purpose – to explain how or why something happens.

> Sometimes you may know more about the age or interests of your reader

Content and organization

- **title** often asks a question, or says clearly what the explanation is about
- text often opens with **general statement(s)** to introduce important words or ideas
- the process is then written in a **series of logical steps**, usually in **time order**
- sometimes **picture(s)** or **diagram(s)**

> This happens... then this happens... next...

Language features

- **third person** writing to make the explanation **impersonal and formal**
- written in the **present tense**
- usually **general nouns and pronouns** (not particular people or things)
- **factual descriptive words**, not like the descriptions in a story
- **technical words and phrases** – which you may need to explain to the reader
- words and devices that show **sequence**
- words and devices that show **cause and effect**

> You would say powerful beams, not beautiful bright beams

> Unusual words that go with the topic such as, canine, translucent and wingspan

> You would write about dogs in general, not a particular dog

> First..., next..., finally

> If..., then... This happens because... This means that...

The basic skeleton for making notes is a flowchart

> The explanation skeleton can change depending on the sort of process

An example of an explanation text

Roman baths

The Romans kept clean and took exercise because they wanted to stay healthy. They built bath-houses in towns, villas and army forts all over Britain, often with sports centres close by.

How were Roman baths heated?

Roman bath-houses were heated by an invention called a hypocaust. This worked by sending hot air underneath the bath-house floor and through hollow channels in the walls, called 'flues'.

Stoking the furnace

The air was heated by a furnace built next to the outer wall of the bath-house. Slaves kept the furnace-fires burning. In Britain, they used brushwood as fuel.

Through the hypocaust

As the fire burned, the draught created by the flues 'pulled' the hot air from the furnace under the bath-house floors and up through the walls. Then it escaped outside along with smoke from the burning wood.

Steam cleaning

As the hot air flowed through the hypocaust, it gave up some of its heat, and the bath-house floor became hot. The bathers splashed water onto the hot floor to make the steam that helped them sweat and get clean.

Cooling off

The rooms next to the furnace were the hottest, because the air flowing under their floors was full of heat from the fire. The rooms further away from the furnace were cooler because the air from the furnace had lost a lot of its heat by the time it reached their floors.

The pool

The pool in the hot room was filled with warm water from a tank set into the floor. The bottom of the tank was heated from underneath by hot air, just like the bath-house floor. When the water in the tank became warm, it rose to the top of the pool. When the water in the pool cooled, it dropped to the bottom of the tank.

Language features and style of the explanation text

- Past tense throughout (as this is historical)
- Style formal, factual
- Time connectives
- Causal connectives

Technical vocabulary to ensure clarity

Technical word explained

Specific noun (type of fuel)

Sentence opening to create cause and effect

Causal connective used to join clauses within sentences to explain relationship between events

Question to focus the reader on explanation

Use of third person

General noun

Device to show cause and effect

Words and devices to signal time

Roman baths

The Romans kept clean and took exercise because they wanted to stay healthy. They built bath-houses in towns, villas and army forts all over Britain, often with a sports centre close by.

How were Roman baths heated?

Roman bath-houses were heated by an invention called a hypocaust. This worked by sending hot air underneath the bath-house floor and through hollow channels in the walls, called 'flues'.

Stoking the furnace

The air was heated by a furnace built next to the outer wall of the bath-house. Slaves kept the furnace-fires burning. In Britain, they used brushwood as fuel.

Through the hypocaust

As the fire burned, the draught created by the flues 'pulled' the hot air from the furnace under the bath-house floors and up through the walls. Then it escaped outside along with smoke from the burning wood.

Steam cleaning

As the hot air flowed through the hypocaust, it gave up some of its heat, and the bath-house floor became hot. The bathers splashed water onto the hot floor to make the steam that helped them sweat and get clean.

Cooling off

The rooms next to the furnace were the hottest, because the air flowing under their floors was full of heat from the fire. The rooms further away from the furnace were cooler because the air from the furnace had lost a lot of its heat by the time it reached their floors.

The pool

The pool in the hot room was filled with warm water from a tank set into the floor. The bottom of the tank was heated from underneath by hot air, just like the bath-house floor. When the water in the tank became warm, it rose to the top of the pool. When the water in the pool cooled, it dropped to the bottom of the tank.

If you are using this text with other year groups, then also highlight these features:

Y4 /P5 ◆ Formal tone
        ◆ Causal language and punctuation
        ◆ How sentences in paragraphs move from the general to the specific to extend explanation
        ◆ Use of sub-headings e.g. **Stoking the furnace; Steam cleaning**

Y5/P6   ◆ The use of impersonal style e.g. **bathers**
        ◆ Useful words and phrases that make sequential or causal links e.g **As, when, because** – point out where they are used as subordinating conjunctions within complex sentences.

Y6/P7   ◆ Develop pupils' understanding of the active and passive and the use of third person in explanations e.g. **The air was heated by the furnace**

Content and organization of the explanation text

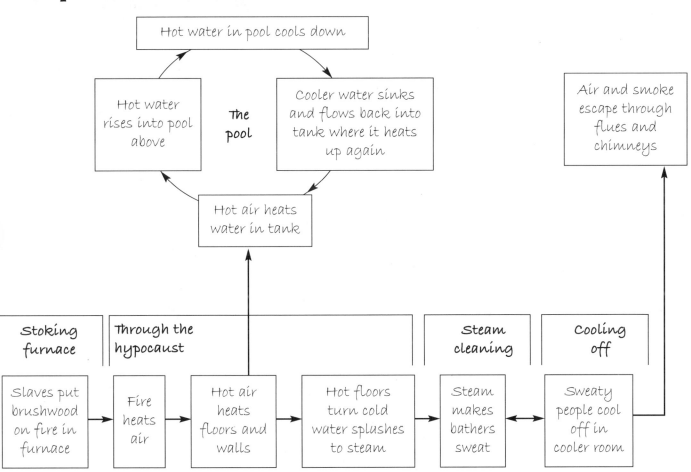

Teaching pupils how to read and write an instruction text

Page 16	Page 17
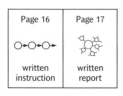	
written instruction	written report

Reading an instruction text

Read pp 16–17 of *Roman Britain* with the pupils. You will need:

- the written instructions on p 16 (the text-only version on p 39 of these notes can be enlarged/ photocopied/made into an OHT for annotation);
- p 38 of these notes which can be enlarged/photocopied/ made into an OHT for annotation.

Audience and purpose

> **SHARED READING ACTIVITY**

Note how the intended audience and purpose affects the language and layout.

Audience – adults/pupils who want to know how to make a Celtic torc.

Purpose – to enable someone to make a torc by following a set of commands in a logical order.

Content and organization

> **SHARED WRITING ACTIVITY**

Show pupils how the content of the written instructions is organized by showing its content as an instruction skeleton (see p 41 of these notes).

Point out that the title includes the phrase 'How to' which clearly suggests which type of text this is, and that each 'step' is marked by a number to aid clarity and to highlight the order in which the procedure should be followed.

The items needed are listed for ease of reading, remembering and collecting in advance. They are in a separate box to indicate to the reader that they are not part of the step-by-step instructions.

An explanation is included to give the reader additional information about the torc and the picture shows the reader the final product.

Language features and style

> **SHARED READING ACTIVITY**

Return to the text and talk about the way language has been used to achieve the effects the author intended (see annotated version on p 40 of these notes).

Point out:
- imperative verbs in the present tense e.g. *measure, roll, twist, arrange*;
- short simple sentences e.g. *add patterns using the modelling tool* for clarity and precision;
- adverbs and adjectives used sparingly to ensure clarity e.g. *carefully, very loosely, curved*;
- details added e.g. *dimensions*, to ensure accuracy.

> **INDEPENDENT ACTIVITIES**

Pupils use these instructions to make a torc to fit themselves.

In a plenary, they could evaluate the effectiveness of the instructions and add in any additional steps or details to enhance clarity.

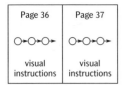
Writing an instruction text

Use pp 36–37 of *Roman Britain* as a basis for pupils' own instruction texts. You will need:

◆ the visual instructions on pp 36–37;

◆ p 38 of these notes enlarged/photocopied/made into an OHT for annotation.

SHARED READING ACTIVITY

Content and organization

Revise the content and organization of the instruction text from the previous session (see p 41 of these notes.)

Pairs of pupils discuss the visual instruction on pp 36–37 of the pupils' book and make instruction skeleton notes. Remind pupils to include in their skeleton any tips they may have noted down when they made the Roman board game e.g. *different designs for the counters.*

Language features and style

Remind pupils of the language features and style of instruction text (see p 38 of these notes).

Audience and purpose

Discuss the audience for pupils' instructions (other pupils/readers who want to know how to make a board game), and the purpose (to tell people the best procedure to follow when making the board game).

Demonstrate how to write the first step, based on the picture in the first box. Remind pupils to put in a short introduction, list the equipment needed and then proceed with the instructions. For example:

How to make a Roman board game
To make the game you will need:
card (16 cm x 16 cm)
modelling clay in three different colours
ruler
pencil
plastic knife
rolling pin

   1. *Take the modelling clay and roll out flat on the card until it is square with each side about 14 cm in length.*

   2. *Use the ruler and the knife to mark out a square on the clay with each side exactly 12 cm in length.*

Discuss the use of time connectives e.g. *until.*

INDEPENDENT WRITING ACTIVITY

Pupils, using their skeleton notes, continue to write the instructions based on the pictures in the correct order. They could also re-write the rules about how to play the game, in their own words.

INDEPENDENT ACTIVITY

Pupils make and play the Roman board game following the visual instructions on pp 36–37 of the pupils' book.

About instruction text

Audience and purpose

Audience – someone who needs to use the instructions.

Purpose – to tell someone how to do or make something.

> Sometimes you may know more about the age or interests of your reader

Content and organization

- **title** (or opening sentence) tells what is to be done or made
- **list** of what is needed

> How to make a . . .

> You will need: 2 sheets of A4 white paper, coloured pens . . . etc

- sometimes **picture(s) or diagram(s)**
- the instructions are written as a sequence in **time order**

> 1. Draw a person . . .
> 2. Cut it out . . .

Language features

- written in the **imperative,** as if the writer is talking directly to the reader telling him or her what to do
- numbers or words and devices to show the **sequence** of the steps
- all **necessary detail** included (for instance, *how many, how far, how long*)
- **factual descriptive words,** not like the descriptions in a story

> Draw a person . . .
> Cut it out . . .

> First . . . next . . . Finally . . .

> 2 A4 sheets of white paper

> NOT two lovely sheets of clean, crisp, white paper!

The basic skeleton for making notes is a flowchart

An example of an instruction text

How to make a torc

Torcs were heavy rings, made of gold, silver or other valuable metals. Celtic people wore them round their necks. The Celts believed torcs had magic powers to protect them from harm. Celtic warriors sometimes fought wearing torcs and body-paint – but nothing else!

You will need:
tape measure
pencil and paper
modelling clay
modelling tool
gold or silver paint
paintbrush

1. Measure the distance round your neck, very loosely. Write down the measurement.

2. Roll out two or three strands of modelling clay (about 10 cm longer than your neck measurement).

3. Twist the strands together carefully.

4. Shape each end of the twisted strands into a loop, a disc or a ball.

5. Add patterns using the modelling tool.

6. Arrange your torc in a curved shape. Do not bring the ends too close together, or you will not be able to put it on.

7. Wait for it to harden.

8. Paint your torc gold or silver, and leave in a warm place to dry.

Language features and style of the instruction text

How to make a torc

Torcs were heavy rings, made of gold, silver or other valuable metals. Celtic people wore them round their necks. The Celts believed torcs had magic powers to protect them from harm. Celtic warriors sometimes fought wearing torcs and body-paint – but nothing else!

General introduction (optional)

You will need:
tape measure
pencil and paper
modelling clay
modelling tool
gold or silver paint
paintbrush

Imperative present tense

Dimensions added to ensure accuracy

Short simple sentences to keep writing clear

Numbers to indicate the sequence in which to carry out instructions

1. Measure the distance round your neck, very loosely. Write down the measurement.

2. Roll out two or three strands of modelling clay (about 10 cm longer than your neck measurement).

3. Twist the strands together carefully.

4. Shape each end of the twisted strands into a loop, a disc or a ball.

5. Add patterns using the modelling tool.

6. Arrange your torc in a curved shape. Do not bring the ends too close together, or you will not be able to put it on.

7. Wait for it to harden.

8. Paint your torc gold or silver, and leave in a warm place to dry.

Adverbs used to ensure clarity and precision by telling the reader the manner in which to carry out the instruction

Addresses the reader generally rather than specifically by naming them

Side notes (left column)
- Present tense throughout
- Imperative form of the verb
- Generic participant rather than named individual
- Formal factual style
- Chronological
- Short clear sentences

If you are using this text with other year groups, then also highlight these features:

Y4/P5
- Use of second person verbs
- Presentational devices i.e. **bullet points** or **numbers, lists, pictures** or **diagrams, boxes**.
- Compare adverbs between instructional and fictional writing

Y5/P6
- Discuss use of 3rd person when writing instructions for more than one player e.g. **player A; player B**
- Test instructions out for their effectiveness, evaluate their usefulness and make the necessary modifications
- Look at other instructional texts and compare how they vary e.g **recipes**
- Draw pupils' attention to the explanation about the purpose of torcs in the introduction

Content and organization of the instruction text

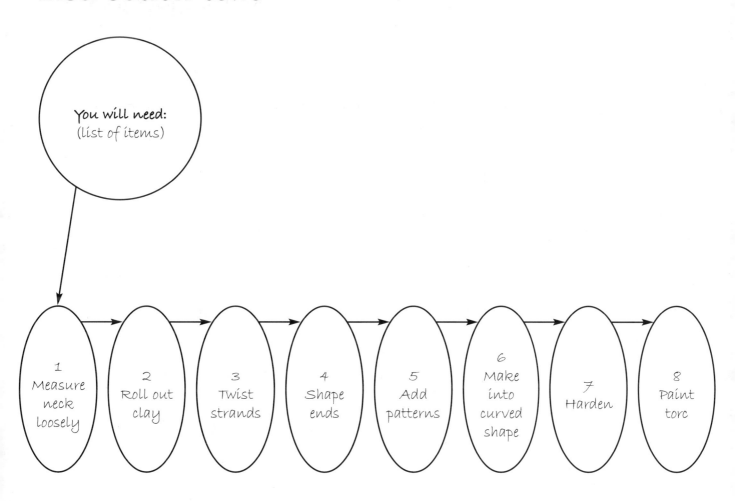

You will need:
(list of items)

1 Measure neck loosely

2 Roll out clay

3 Twist strands

4 Shape ends

5 Add patterns

6 Make into curved shape

7 Harden

8 Paint torc

Teaching pupils how to read and write recount text

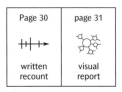

Page 30	page 31
written recount	visual report

Reading a recount text in a letter

Read pp 30–31 of *Roman Britain* with the pupils. You will need:

- The written recount on p 30 (the text-only version on p 45 of these notes can be enlarged/ photocopied/made into an OHT for annotation);
- p 44 of these notes which can be enlarged/photocopied/made into an OHT for annotation.

Audience and purpose

> **SHARED READING ACTIVITY**

Note how the intended audience and purpose affects the language and layout.

Audience – Celtic prince's parents.

Purpose – to tell of his safe arrival and recount the events on the first day at the villa.

Content and organization

> **SHARED WRITING ACTIVITY**

Identify key phrases in the letter and show pupils how the content of this written recount is organized by showing its content as a report skeleton (see p 47 of these notes).

Point out that the text recounts the events of the journey and then follows with a description of the villa itself. This is supported by a change of tense from past – paragraphs 1 and 2 (recounting the events of yesterday) – and the present – paragraph 3 (what the villa is like). It is organized into longer and shorter paragraphs each focusing on a different event.

Show pupils how to summarize the stages of the recount by text-marking key words and phrases. Pupils could use paired talk, giving an oral summary of the text-marked items before writing their own skeleton notes.

Language features and style

> **SHARED READING ACTIVITY**

Return to the written recount text and talk about the way language has been used to achieve the effects the author intended (see annotated version on p 46 of these notes). Point out:

- the use of the past tense – since the events have already happened, and the contrasting use of the present tense in paragraph 3 to describe the villa is used;
- notice how first person is used and how this related to the intended audience;
- look at the use of time connectives e.g. *yesterday, when, this afternoon, then;* adjectives e.g. *enormous, wet, smelly, steep, grand, proud,* that add detail for the reader.

> **INDEPENDENT ACTIVITY**

Pupils describe a journey they have made and recount this to a partner in a speaking and listening activity. After this discussion, each pupil creates their own recount skeleton notes of events on their journey.

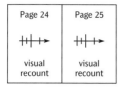

Page 24	Page 25
┼┼┼→	┼┼┼→
visual recount	visual recount

Writing a recount in a letter

Use pp 24–25 of *Roman Britain* as a basis for pupils' own recount texts. You will need:
- ◆ the visual recount on pp 24–25;
- ◆ p 44 of these notes enlarged/photocopied/made into an OHT for annotation.

Content and organization

> SHARED READING ACTIVITY

Revise the content and organization of the recount text from the previous session (see p 47 of these notes.)

In pairs, pupils discuss the visual recount on pp 24–25 of the pupils' book.

Groups of pupils use role play to enact events described in the visual recount in a series of still pictures. A narrator describes the sequence of events.

> SHARED WRITING ACTIVITY

Pupils then make skeleton notes from the visual recount on pp 24–25.

Tell pupils they are going to write a letter recounting the events of the Iceni rebellion and Boudicca's death. Pairs of pupils use skeletons to retell the events.

Language features and style

Return to the text and remind pupils of the language features and style of recounts (see p 44 of these notes) and the organization of letters.

Audience and purpose

Discuss the audience for the recount (relations of the letter writer who know nothing about the Iceni tribe and Boudicca) and the purpose (to retell the events of the Iceni rebellion and Boudicca's death).

> SHARED WRITING ACTIVITY

Demonstrate writing a short introductory paragraph of about three sentences imitating some of the sentence constructions in the villa letter, for example:

Dear Mum and Dad,

Our fight ended yesterday. It was the most difficult and dangerous fight I have ever taken part in. We were fighting the Iceni tribe. This was a tribe whose leader was a Queen. Her name was Boudicca. She was a very strong leader.

Model the further paragraphs for the pupils, referring to their skeletons to discuss contents and events e.g.:

She and her tribe had attacked Verulanium and had set fire to Londinium. She was threatening Roman rule here in Britannia. Something had to be done.

Discuss how to add extra detail and personal thoughts e.g.

I saw her die in front of her last warriors. I couldn't quite believe she would do that. Her words to me as she lay dying were "I'd rather die than be captured!" I rather admired her.

> INDEPENDENT WRITING ACTIVITY

Pupils write their own letter using the paragraph modelled as a starter, if necessary.

⊬⊢⊣→ About recount text

Audience and purpose

Audience – someone who may not know much about the events.

Purpose – to retell events that actually happened.

Sometimes you may know more about the age or interests of your reader

Content and organization

- **introductory paragraph** sets the scene, so the reader has all the basic facts needed to understand the recount
- **introduction** often also hints at the main event of the recount
- events written in **chronological order** – time order
- **closing statement** – sentence(s) or paragraph to bring the recount to an end

Answers the questions *who? what? when? where?*

First this happened ... then this happened ... next ...

Use your introductory sentence to help you write your conclusion. If the introduction is a question then answer it in your conclusions

Language features

- written in the **past tense** because these are specific events that only happened once
- focus on **specific people, places, dates** etc.
- may be written in the **first** or **third person**
- **words and devices** to show **time order**

This usually means proper nouns, so remember the capital letters!

Stick to one or the other – don't mix them up

First ..., next ..., finally ..., In 1950 ..., Some weeks later ...

The basic skeleton for making notes is a timeline

Example of a recount text in a letter

A Roman Villa
Fishbourne
Sussex

Dear Mum and Dad

I got to the villa yesterday. The journey took two whole days. When we arrived, all dirty, a bossy slave made me go to the bath-house. There was a room full of steam, where the slave wiped all the mud off me, and a huge pool of warm water to swim in. Then I met the other two boys who are Celtic princes like me. We've got to learn about Roman ways, and how to speak Latin.

The villa is enormous. It has sixty different rooms! It's made of stone, and there are huge pillars – as big as tree-trunks – holding up the roof. Inside, the floors are covered with pictures made of tiny bits of coloured clay. The walls are painted with pictures too, and there are stone statues everywhere – they remind me of ghosts. There's a garden, with a fountain, right in the middle of the villa!

After exploring the house, we went outside. They have rooms for horses, called 'stables', cattle-sheds, barns full of grain and hay, and big brick buildings where the slaves sleep. They have fruit trees in the garden – the Romans don't pick wild fruit, like us – and lots of herbs and vegetables, growing in neat rows. We noticed plants with strange purple and orange roots which the Romans brought from Italy. I think they are called carrots. Do you think they will be safe to eat?

At dinner, there were funny wooden things to sit on, called chairs, and beds on legs, called couches. The grown-up Romans lay down on them to eat their meals. The food was cooked in a separate room called a kitchen. After dark, they set fire to oil in little pots to make the room bright. And I noticed another strange thing – all the floors felt hot!

The teacher has called us to our lessons, so I must go now.

Your loving son
Caratacus (prince)

Language features and style of recount text in a letter

A Roman Villa
Fishbourne
Sussex

Dear Mum and Dad

I got to the villa yesterday. The journey took two whole days. When we arrived, all dirty, a bossy slave made me go to the bath-house. There was a room full of steam, where the slave wiped all the mud off me, and a huge pool of warm water to swim in. Then I met the other two boys who are Celtic princes like me. We've got to learn about Roman ways, and how to speak Latin.

The villa is enormous. It has sixty different rooms! It's made of stone, and there are huge pillars – as big as tree-trunks – holding up the roof. Inside, the floors are covered with pictures made of tiny bits of coloured clay. The walls are painted with pictures too, and there are stone statues everywhere – they remind me of ghosts. There's a garden, with a fountain, right in the middle of the villa!

After exploring the house, we went outside. They have rooms for horses, called 'stables', cattle-sheds, barns full of grain and hay, and big brick buildings where the slaves sleep. They have fruit trees in the garden – the Romans don't pick wild fruit, like us – and lots of herbs and vegetables, growing in neat rows. We noticed plants with strange purple and orange roots which the Romans brought from Italy. I think they are called carrots. Do you think they will be safe to eat?

At dinner, there were funny wooden things to sit on, called chairs, and beds on legs, called couches. The grown-up Romans lay down on them to eat their meals. The food was cooked in a separate room called a kitchen. After dark, they set fire to oil in little pots to make the room bright. And I noticed another strange thing – all the floors felt hot!

The teacher has called us to our lessons, so I must go now.

Your loving son
Caratacus (prince)

Annotations:

- Writing organized in paragraphs each dealing with a different aspect of the recount
- First person, link to audience of the letter – parents
- Specific people
- Shift to present tense in report describing villa as it is.
- Adjectives used to describe and give detail
- Letter writer's name
- Letter writer's address
- Audience – people letter is written to
- Verbs past tense in recount
- Time connectives that join and sequence events
- Detail to add interest to reader
- Question to involve reader
- Closing statement

If you are using this text with other year groups, then also highlight these features:

Y4 /P5 ◆ The use of powerful verbs, adjectives and adverbs to convey events clearly to the reader e.g. **bossy, enormous** – discuss alternatives
◆ How to sequence ideas correctly and discuss how to choose one or two events to add more detail to the writing
◆ The use of a simile e.g **as big as tree-trunks**, to portray exact dimensions
◆ Choice of correct tenses for report or explanation within a recount.

Y5/P6 ◆ The use of sentence and time connectives to move the recount forward e.g **as, after** – discuss how these can be changed to avoid repetition
◆ Look at the use of different verb tenses to create different effects e.g in **report** about villa; **question** about carrots etc.
◆ Use parts of the letter to write a report text describing the features of a villa.

Y6/P7 ◆ How recounts can be written as autobiographies and biographies (refer to pp 20–21 of the pupils' book)
◆ Focus on the use of subjective and objective references (e.g. **they remind me of ghosts, roots … brought from Italy**) in biographies and autobiographies and discuss why these differ.

Content and organization of the recount text in the letter

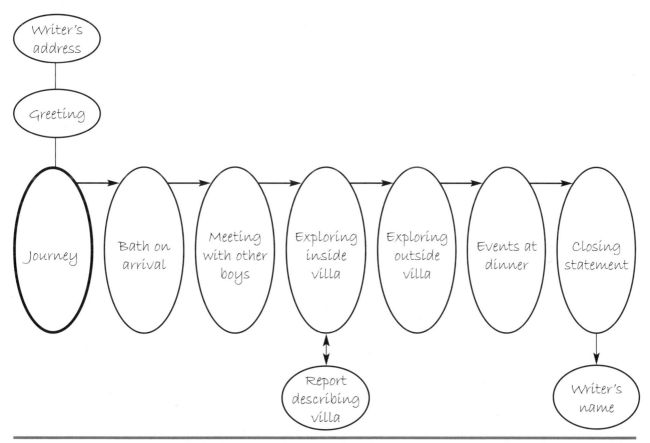

Page	Contents	Text Type	National Literacy Strategy Objectives	QCA History Objectives Unit 6a
				Pupils should learn:
2	Concept map Contents	Reference	T3 17	
4	What do we know about the Romans?	Written report	T1 TL 19, 20, 21, 22 T1 SL 1, 4, 9 T1 WL 13, 14	• to use the terms 'invade' and 'settle' • to place the Celtic and Roman periods in a chronological framework • to recognise characteristics that place Celts and Romans as having lived a long time ago in the past • that Romans invaded Britain and that the period of conquest was followed by a period of settlement
6	The Roman Empire (map)	Visual report	T1 TL 19, 20, 21, 22 T1 SL 9, 10 T1 WL 13, 14	
8	Roman times	Visual recount	T3 TL 19, 22, 25, 26 T3 SL 1, 2, 3, 5, 6 T3 WL 6, 12	
10	World beaters	Visual report	T1 TL 19, 20 T1 SL 9, 10 T1 WL 13, 14	
12	Clothes and weapons	Visual report	T1 TL 19, 20, 21, 22 T1 SL 1, 4, 9, 10, 11, 12 T1 WL 6, 13, 14	• to make comparisons between these lifestyles • about aspects of life in Celtic and Roman Britain, using a variety of resources
14	Britain before the Romans	Written report Visual report	T1 TL 19, 20, 21 T1 SL 1, 4, 9 T1 WL 13, 14	• about aspects of life in Celtic and Roman Britain, using a variety of resources
16	How to make a torc	Written instructions Written report	T2 TL 12, 13, 14, 15 T2 SL 1, 6, 7, 8, 9, 10 T2 WL 17, 18	• to make comparisons between these lifestyles • about aspects of life in Celtic and Roman Britain, using a variety of resources
18	A Celtic farm	Visual report	T1 TL 19, 20, 21, 22 T1 SL 9, 10 T1 WL 13, 14 T3 TL 20	
20	I came, I saw, I conquered!	Written recount	T3 TL 19, 22, 25, 26 T3 SL 1, 2, 3, 5, 6 T3 WL 6, 12	• to use the terms 'invade' and 'settle' • to place the Celtic and Roman periods in a chronological framework
22	Roman conquest of Britain	Visual recount	T3 TL 19, 22, 25, 26 T3 SL 1, 2, 3, 5, 6 T3 WL 6, 12	• to use the terms 'invade' and 'settle' • to place the Celtic and Roman periods in a chronological framework
24	Boudicca	Visual recount	T3 TL 19, 22, 25, 26 T3 SL 1, 2, 3, 5, 6 T3 WL 6, 12	• that there are different opinions about Boudicca • the main events in Boudicca's revolt • the reason for the revolt • that there are different interpretations of the revolt • about the results of Boudicca's revolt
26	Boudicca – Was she right or wrong?	Visual discussion		
28	Explore Roman Britain	Visual report	T1 TL 19, 20, 21 T1 SL 9, 10 T1 WL 13, 14	• about evidence that tells us about life in Roman Britain
30	My visit to a villa	Written recount Visual report	T3 TL 19, 22, 25, 26 T3 SL 1, 2, 3, 5, 6 T3 WL 6, 12	• about aspects of life in Celtic and Roman Britain, using a variety of resources • about evidence that tells us about life in Roman Britain • ask and answer questions about what survived from the Roman settlement of Britain
32	Roman roads	Visual explanation	T2 TL 16, 17 T2 SL 9 T2 WL 6, 17, 18	
34	Roman baths	Written explanation Visual explanation	T2 TL 17 T2 SL 1, 6, 8, 9 T2 WL 17, 18	
36	Make a Roman board game	Visual instructions	T2 TL 12, 13, 14, 15, 16, 17 T2 SL 1, 6, 7, 8, 9, 10 T2 WL 6, 17, 18,	• about aspects of life in Celtic and Roman Britain, using a variety of resources
38	Temples and tombs	Written report	T1 TL 19, 20, 21, 22 T1 SL 1, 4, 9 T1 WL 13, 14	• about aspects of life in Celtic and Roman Britain, using a variety of resources • about evidence that tells us about life in Roman Britain
40	Meet some Roman Britons	Written report	T1 TL 19, 20, 21 T1 SL 1, 4, 9 T1 WL 13, 14	• about aspects of life in Celtic and Roman Britain, using a variety of resources • about evidence that tells us about life in Roman Britain
42	Roman rule – good or bad?	Written discussion	T2 TL 17	
44	Why did the Romans leave Britain?	Written explanation	T2 TL 17 T2 SL 1, 6, 8, 9 T2 WL 17, 18	
46	Glossary	Reference	T1 WL 14 T2 WL 23 T3 TL 17	
47	Bibliography	Reference	T1 WL 14, 15 T2 WL 23 T3 TL 17	
48	Index	Reference	T1 WL 14 T2 WL 23 T3 TL 17	